My Monarch Journal

By _____
Your Name

and Connie Muther

Photographs by Anita Bibeau

Student Edition
also available
(does not include
Parent-Teacher section,
pages 32-51)

To Garry~
May you continue
to sail through oceans
of air ~ Like the Monarch.
Thanks so much for
sharing so many
things with us.
Hugs, Connie Muther
& Rich Ernst :)

Dawn Publications

Table of Contents

Introduction

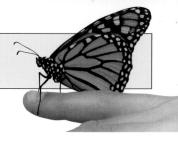

THIS IS YOUR BOOK. *You* are the author. This is a science journal. *You* are the scientist.

Over a period of about three or four weeks, you will observe a miracle of nature called ***metamorphosis*** (pronounced **met-ah-MOR-fa-sis**). It's a huge word with a huge meaning. It means a complete change of form. You will watch a Monarch completely change its form—several times! This is one of the best examples of metamorphosis in the world.

This is *your* journal in which to record the changes in *your* Monarch. Watch it carefully. Every Monarch is different, just as every person is different. Your Monarch may not grow as fast or as slow as ours. Yours may not look exactly like ours. But, like all Monarchs, yours will eat and grow and change completely. Draw or write about what you see, hear, feel, and think. Think about how Monarchs change over their lifetime. Think about their changes as compared with the changes that happen in other animals and humans as they grow. Ask questions—lots of questions, just like a scientist. You will find some answers, and sometimes you will not—just as scientists sometimes find answers and sometimes do not.

This science log begins with a newly laid Monarch egg. If you start with a caterpillar rather than an egg, that's OK. Just compare your caterpillar with our pictures, start where you think your caterpillar is and then go forward. Even if you don't have a caterpillar at all, that's OK, too. Just pretend that ours is yours. Examine our pictures, write your notes or draw pictures below, and when you've finished this book you'll know a lot about Monarchs—and metamorphosis!

Anita and Connie begin.

_____ begins.
                    your name

Day: _____   Time: _____

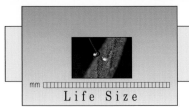

mm
Life Size

| A. What's the little white bump? | B. What a funny place for an egg! Why put it there? | C. How is it changing? | D. A head pops out! Hello world! | E. How does it get out? |

Draw and/or write about what you see.

The First Meal

A.	B.	C.	D.	E.
What a tight squeeze!	What is it doing with the egg case?	Did it make those holes?	Oh-oh! Is that little dark blob what I think it is? Why is its body green?	Is it a boy or a girl? Nobody knows! We named ours Monty. Have you named yours?

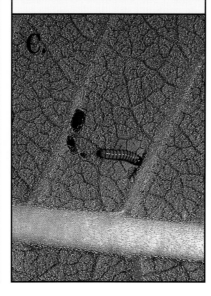

Day 1

5

Life Size - Day 2

Wow! How can she grow so fast?

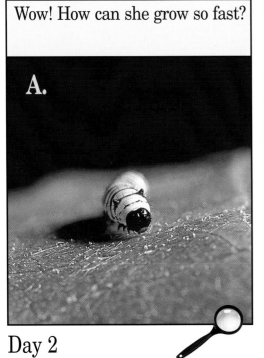

A.

Day 2

Look, her face is different! What is that black thing?

B.

Day 3

How big is Monty now?

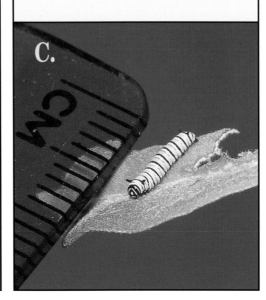

C.

Day 4

What are those floppy things on her body?

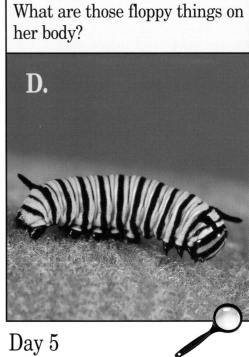

D.

Day 5

Eating, Pooping, Walking–and Swinging!

How much does Monty eat?

A.

Day 6

Oh-oh! Does she poop much?

B.

Day 6

How can she walk upside-down?

C.

Day 7

Does she ever fall off?

D.

Day 7

Preparing to Molt

Can you make out a new head under Monty's skin?

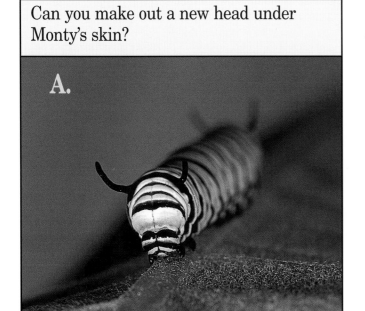

A.

Day 8   5:00 P.M.

Can you see wrinkled new skin under her old skin?

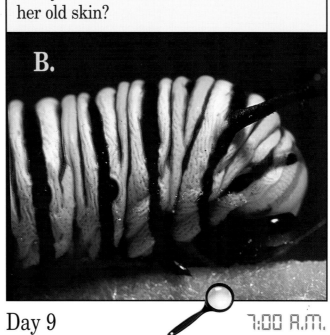

B.

Day 9   7:00 A.M.

More changes to her head!

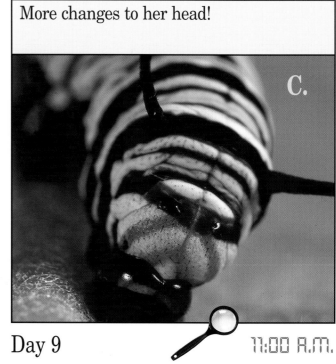

C.

Day 9   11:00 A.M.

8

Stretch! Watch Monty and her friend below.	She bursts out!	What's that gray line?	How many legs does she have now?	Watch as she pulls out each wobbly, wet leg!
A.	**B.**	**C.**	**D.**	**E.**

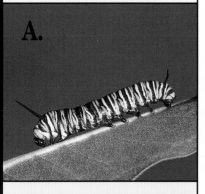  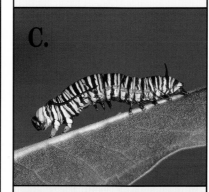  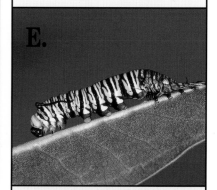

Day 9　　　9:00 P.M.　　　　9:02 P.M.　　　　9:03 P.M.　　　　9:03 P.M.　　　　9:04 P.M.

Finally Free!

Finally! Now, watch Monty's head.	"A new me!"	Here is the old head covering!
A. 	B.	C. 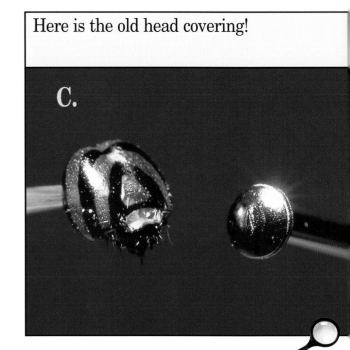

Day 9   9:05 P.M.

The Molted Skin—Yum!

Why are Monty's tentacles shaped like Z's?	What can you see in this old skin?	Turning around and . . .	Yum!

A.
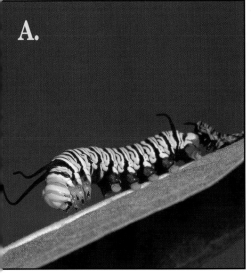

B.

C.
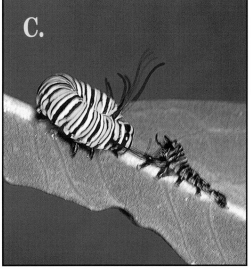

D.
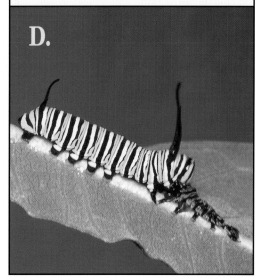

Day 9   9:30 P.M.   9:31 P.M.   10:30 P.M.   10:33 P.M.

The Body Parts

Insects have 3 body parts —abdomen, thorax and head. Where are Monty's?	How many legs does she have?	Does Monty have no privacy?	How many of Monty's "noses" can you see in this picture?	Can you find her last air hole? Can you find the hooks on her rear feet?

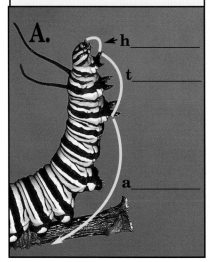

A. h_____ t_____ a_____

B.

C.

D. spiracle

E.

Day 10

Let's Face It–I'm Cute!

Can you see her eyes?	Can you find her antenna?	Smile, Monty!	Can you find the place that produces her silk?	What parts can you see in this molted head?
 A.	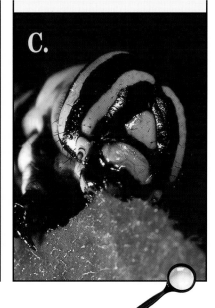 B.	 C.	 D.	 E.

Day 11

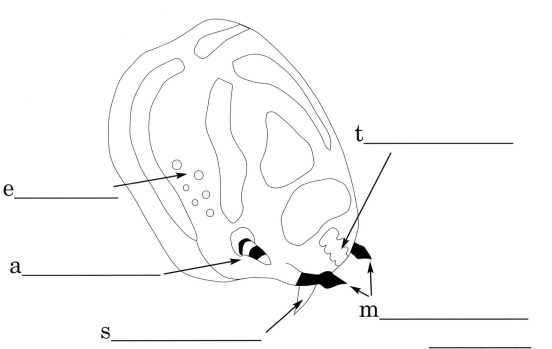

e_____

a_____

s_____

t_____

m_____

_____

Label and color

_____

_____

_____

_____

_____

_____

_____

_____

_____

_____

_____

_____

_____

13

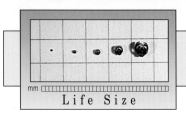
How Old Is Your Caterpillar?

You can't tell how far along caterpillars are by how old they are because they grow at different rates, depending mostly on temperature. Instead, caterpillars are in their "first instar" from the time they hatch until their first molting. They are then in their "second instar" until their second molting, and so on for a total of five instars. The last instar ends when the caterpillar becomes a chrysalis. In diagram form, it goes like this:

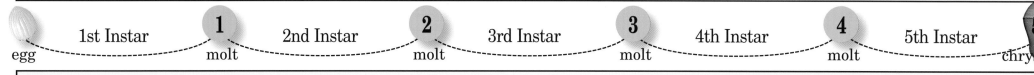

egg — 1st Instar — **1** molt — 2nd Instar — **2** molt — 3rd Instar — **3** molt — 4th Instar — **4** molt — 5th Instar — **5** chrys

The pictures below show Monty in all five instars. The top photos show her face. What differences do you see? The bottom photos show her body. What differences do you see?

2 to 6 mm (1/16 to 1/4 inch)   5 to 10 mm (3/16 to 3/8 inch)   9 to 14 mm (3/8 to 5/8 inch)   13 to 25 mm (1/2 to 1 inch)   24 to 64 mm (1 to 2 1/2 inches)

Why did Monty leave the milkweed and start wandering all over?

A.

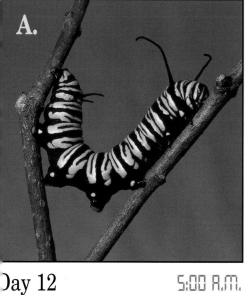

Dead end! What is she looking for?

B.

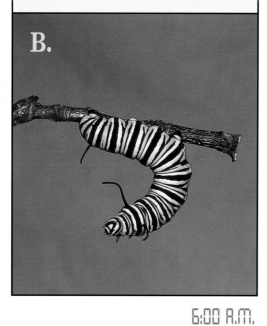

Finally, she stopped—and can you see what she's woven around the twig?

C.

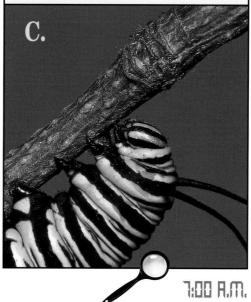

Can you see what she's doing now?

D.

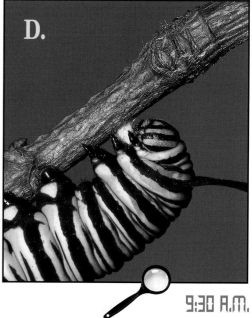

Day 12   5:00 A.M.   6:00 A.M.   7:00 A.M.   9:30 A.M.

15

Creating a White "Button"

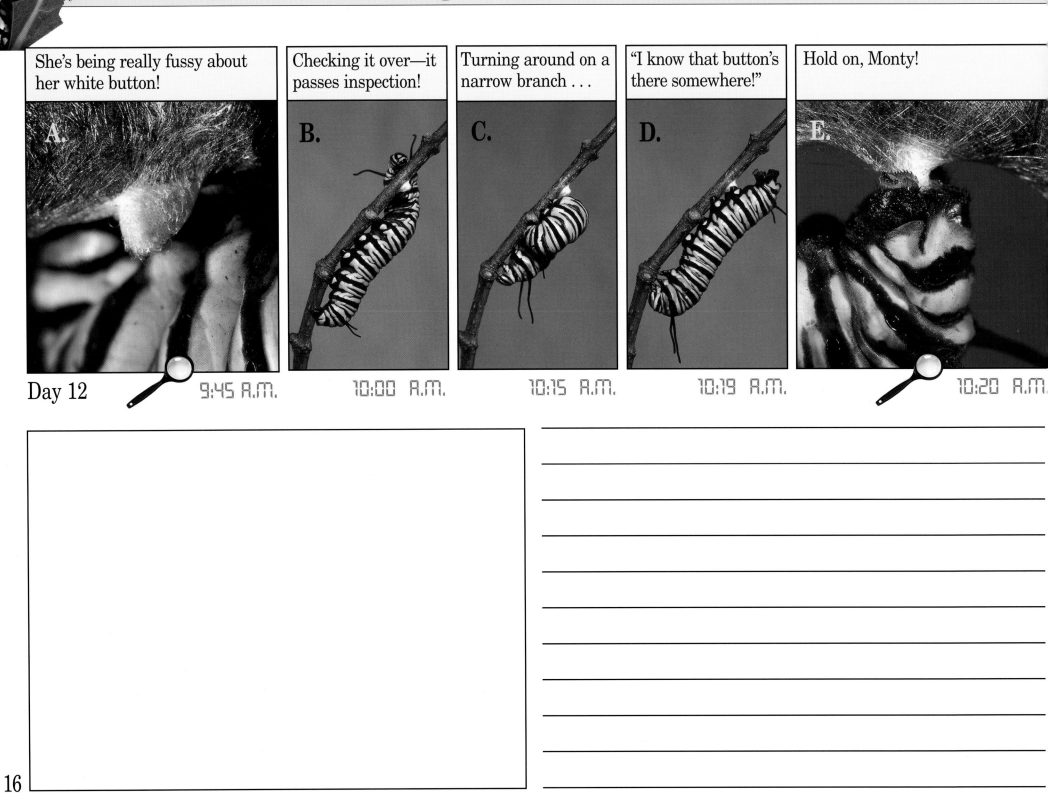

She's being really fussy about her white button!

A.

Day 12   9:45 A.M.

Checking it over—it passes inspection!

B.

10:00 A.M.

Turning around on a narrow branch . . .

C.

10:15 A.M.

"I know that button's there somewhere!"

D.

10:19 A.M.

Hold on, Monty!

E.

10:20 A.M.

Letting Go!

How many feet are holding on?	How many now?	She pushes her head against the branch and . . . whee!
A. 	**B.** 	**C.** 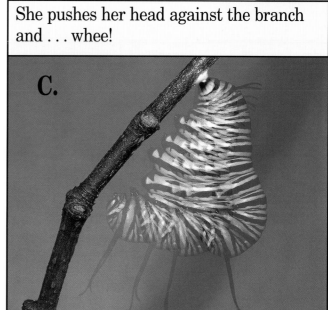

Day 12   1:05 P.M.   2:27 P.M.   2:31 P.M.

Last Hours as a Caterpillar

How long will Monty hang by her feet?

A.

Day 12   2:46 P.M.

She is within 1 to 2 hours of a big change! Do you see what happened?

B.

Day 13   8:20 A.M.

She is within 2 to 30 minutes of the big change! What else is happening?

C.

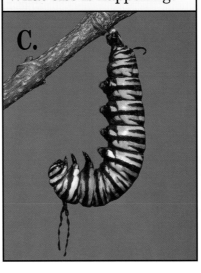

8:30 A.M.

Where is her head now?

D.

8:41 A.M.

Where are her legs going? What's that long line on her side?

E.

8:43 A.M.

18

The Last Molt

Her skin splits!	This molt is like taking off a body suit . . .	with no hands . . .	while hanging from your legs . . .	then changing shoes! (How is she attached to the white "button" now?)

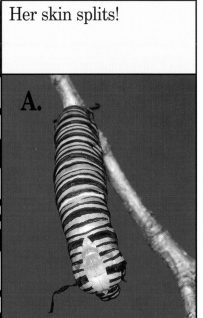    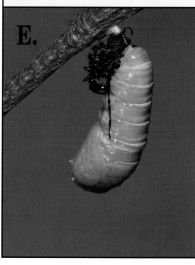

A.   B.   C.   D.   E.

Day 13   8:45 A.M.   8:46 A.M.   8:46 A.M.   8:47 A.M.   8:48 A.M.

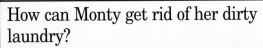

Becoming a Chrysalis

How can Monty get rid of her dirty laundry?

A.

Day 13 8:49 A.M.   8:50 A.M.

Is it a caterpillar? Or a butterfly?

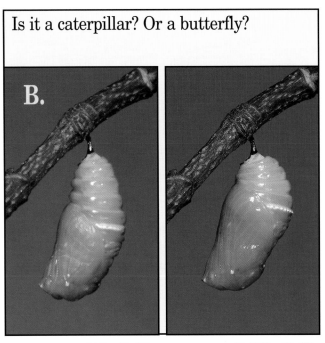

B.

8:52 A.M.   9:05 A.M.

How long does it take?

C.

10:40 A.M.   10:44 A.M.

The Chrysalis–Beautiful and Intriguing

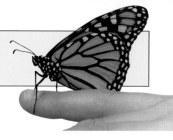

Why does Monty have gold spots and a gold band?

A.

Day 14

Monty is "X-rayed" with sunlight for a minute. How does she breathe?

B.

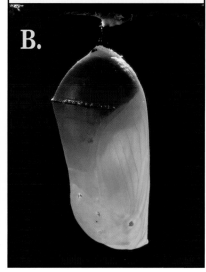

Day 15

How can Monty live without eating?

C.

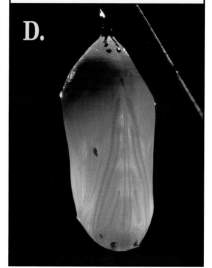

Day 18

Where are her legs, mouth, and head now?

D.

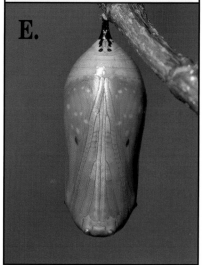

Day 22

Her color is changing! Can you see the wings? Tomorrow is the big day!

E.

Day 23

A Butterfly Is Born

Now she's black and orange! Why?

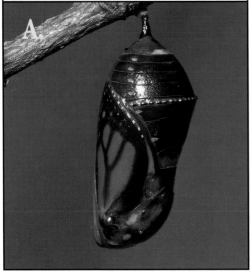

A.

Do you see the notched grooves that have formed? It's time to watch closely!

B.

The casing splits!

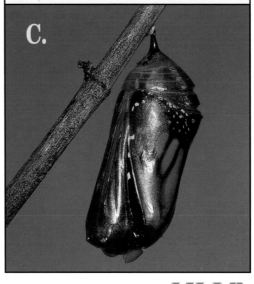

C.

How does she get out?

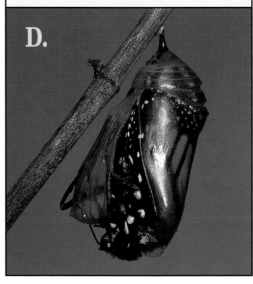

D.

Day 24   11:00 P.M.   Day 25   6:54 A.M.   6:55 A.M.   6:55 A.M.

22

Almost out . . .	Monty, are your feet stuck?	Are her wings on backwards?	Her body is kind of fat, and her wings are kind of short!

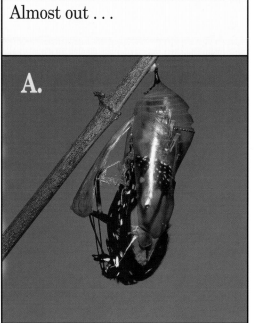

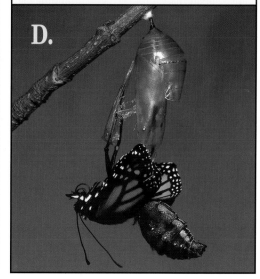

Day 25   6:56 A.M.   6:56 A.M.   6:57 A.M.   6:57 A.M.

The Home Stretch

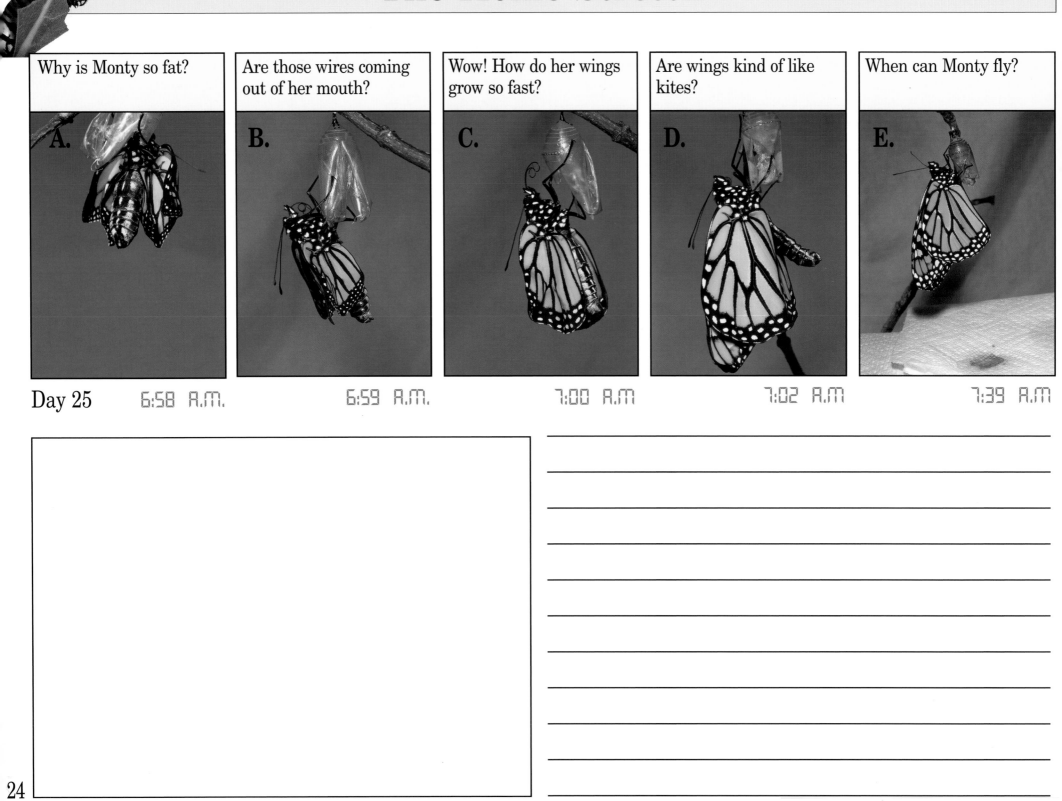

Why is Monty so fat?	Are those wires coming out of her mouth?	Wow! How do her wings grow so fast?	Are wings kind of like kites?	When can Monty fly?
A.	B.	C.	D.	E.

Day 25   6:58 A.M.   6:59 A.M.   7:00 A.M   7:02 A.M   7:39 A.M

Examining Your New Butterfly

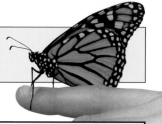

How many wings does Monty have?	Can you count her toes?	Her eyes are very different!	Look at the long wires attached to her head!	Let's look closer. Can you find her scales?

A.

B.

C.

D.

E.
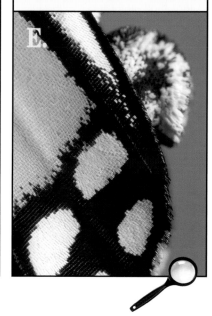

Day 25

25

Releasing Your Butterfly

Finally we can tell—is Monty a boy or girl?

A.

Here's a boy—what is distinctive about him?

B.

Can you find Monty's new head, thorax, abdomen?

C.

When and how should I release my butterfly?

D.

Goodbye Monty! I wonder where she will go?

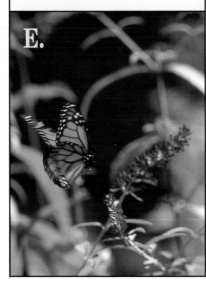
E.

Milkweed—for Breakfast, Lunch and Dinner

Milkweed is the only thing Monarch caterpillars eat! What does it look like?

A.
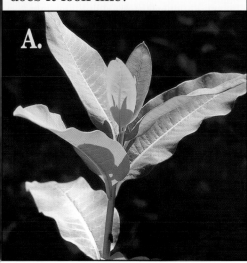

What is that white drop?

B.
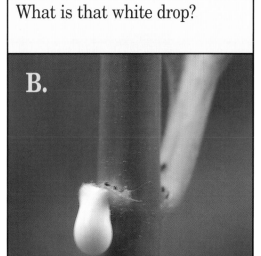

Where can I find it?

C.
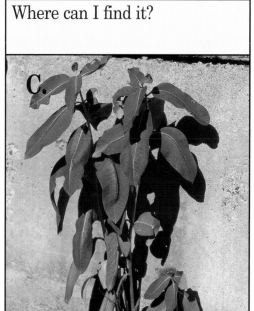

How can I grow it? How can I keep it?

D.
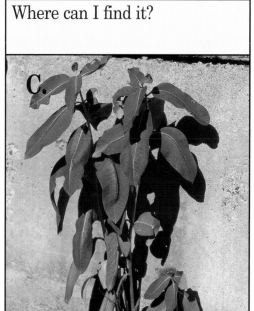

Milkweed Through the Seasons

The bud in spring . . .

the flower . . .

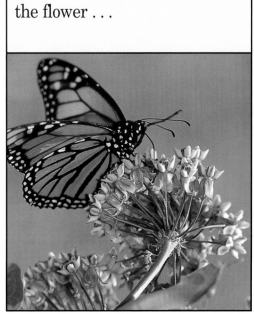

and seed pod in summer . . .

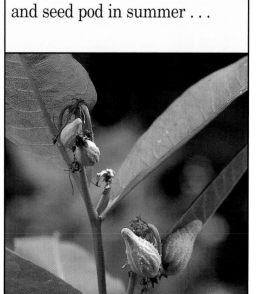

and tufted seeds in fall.

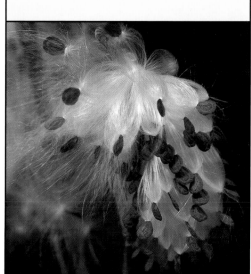

When—and how—can I find Monarch eggs or caterpillars?

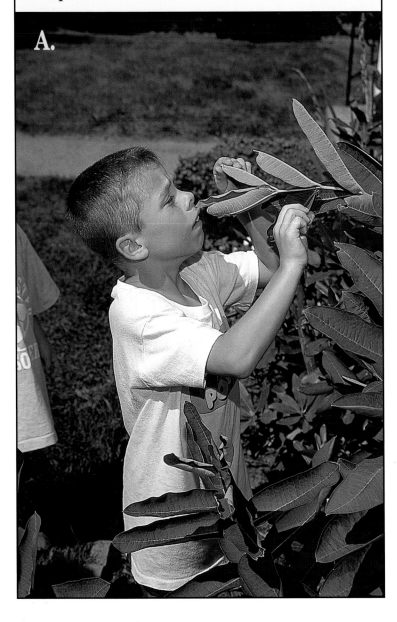

What do I do with the eggs? How do I feed it?

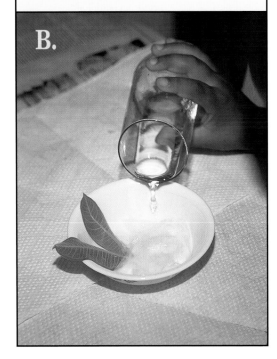

How do I pick up my baby caterpillar? Where should I keep it?

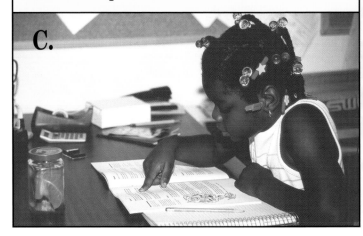

How often should I clean the cage? What should I look for?

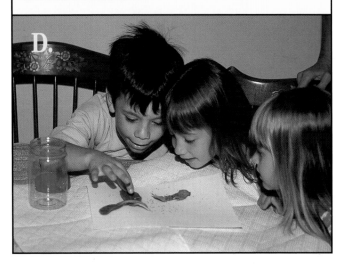

Measuring—and feeding it more and more!

Magnifying glasses and hand lenses are fun . . .

But stereo microscopes are the best! How can I get one?

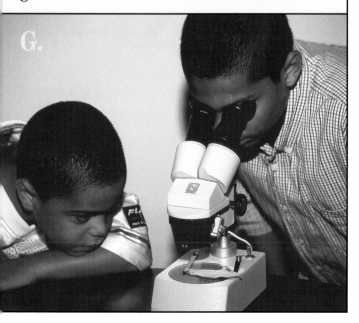

When can I handle my caterpillar?

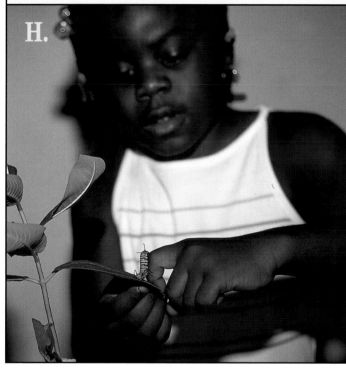

What's the best place for my caterpillar to make a chrysalis?

How about a large cage?

Tracking the Growth of My Monarch

By _____

Your Name

Keep track of the growth of your Monarch caterpillar on this bar graph. Carefully measure the length of your caterpillar with a ruler. Then go to the bottom of the graph and find the number of days you have had your caterpillar. Color in the column until you reach the measurement you have just taken. (If you are measuring in millimeters, look at the scale on the left; if you are measuring in inches, look at the scale on the right.)

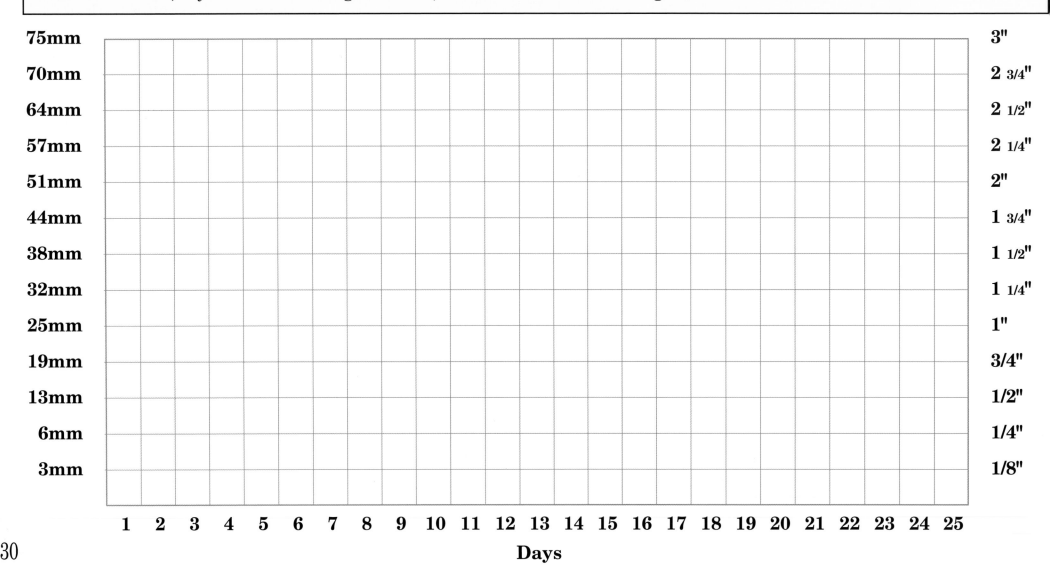

Glossary

Antenna (an-TEN-ah), pl. antennae (an-TEN-ee): Organ on the head of an insect used for feeling, smelling and tasting. (Compare with tentacles which are found on the body, not the head.)

Abdomen (AB-duh-men): The rear part of an insect's body. Ten prolegs support this part of the caterpillar. No legs support this part of the butterfly.

Caterpillar (CAT-er-pill-er): The second stage of a butterfly's four-part life.

Chrysalis (KRIS-ah-lis): The stage when the caterpillar sheds its skin for the last time, and in which the butterfly forms.

Cocoon (kuh-KOON): The silken case formed around the pupa by some moth caterpillars.

Compound eyes (COM-pownd): The eyes of an adult insect composed of thousands of parts, each one of which allows the insect to see in a slightly different direction.

Cremaster (KREE-mas-ter): The black stem with many tiny hooks on its tip that attaches the chrysalis to the silk button spun by the caterpillar.

Crochets (krow-SHAYS): Tiny hooks on the 10 prolegs of a caterpillar.

Cuticle (CUE-ti-cul): The outermost layer of the insect's skin which forms the exoskeleton.

Exoskeleton (ex-o-SKEL-ah-ton): The outer "skeleton" of an insect (insects do not have bones) made of the cuticle.

Frass: The solid waste or excrement of caterpillars and butterflies.

Insect (IN-sekt): An animal with three parts to its body (head, thorax and abdomen), six legs and, usually, wings.

Instar (IN-star): Each caterpillar (larval) stage between molts. With Monarchs, the "first instar" hatches from its egg. There are five instars in the Monarch life cycle. The "fifth instar" ends when it becomes a chrysalis.

Hatchling: A caterpillar just out of the egg and before it has shed its skin. Also called a caterpillar in the first instar.

Larva (LAR-vah) pl. larvae (LAR-vee): The second stage of a butterfly's life. A caterpillar is the larva of a butterfly.

Mandibles (MAN-da-bulz): The jaws of an insect. A caterpillar has five teeth on each mandible. The Monarch caterpillar's mandibles move sideways. A butterfly has no mandibles.

Maxillary palps (MAX-a-lary palps): Sensory structures on either side of the mouth of a caterpillar that help direct food.

Metamorphosis (met-ah-MOR-fa-sis): A complete change from one form to another. Butterflies go through four different forms: egg, larva (caterpillar), pupa (chrysalis), and adult (butterfly). Many insects only have three stages.

Molt: The shedding of an animal's old layer of skin, scales, fur or feathers. Monarch caterpillars molt five times, the last time becoming a chrysalis.

Prolegs (PRO-legs): Stubby, fleshy legs supporting the abdomen of a caterpillar. The Monarch has 10 prolegs, also called false legs. The six "true" legs are part of the thorax.

Proboscis (pro-BOSS-is): The long, coiled sucking tube the butterfly uses for eating its liquid diet.

Pupa (PUE-pa): The transitional stage during which an insect changes into an adult. For a butterfly, the pupa is the chrysalis.

Spinneret (SPIN-ah-ret): The organ that produces silk, part of the lower lip of a caterpillar.

Spiracles (SPIR-a-culz): Round openings for breathing found along the thorax and abdomen. A Monarch has nine pairs.

Tentacles (TEN-ta-culz): Long, flexible extensions on the body of some insects. Monarch tentacles do not have any sense organs. (See antenna). The Monarch caterpillar has four tentacles, one pair on each end. The adult butterfly has no tentacles.

Thorax (THO-rax): The middle section of an insect's body to which the six legs and wings attach.

Trachea (TRAY-kee-ah) pl. tracheae (TRAY-kee): Long tubes that deliver air through the body of an insect. In caterpillars these are attached to the spiracles and are pulled out of the body during molting.

Introduction for Parents and Teachers

Dear Parents and Teachers,

Why did we create this book?

When I was 8, an older friend placed a Monarch caterpillar in my hand and began explaining about the miracle of metamorphosis I was about to witness. I have raised Monarchs ever since. As an educator, I managed to squeeze them into the curriculum no matter what the grade level (K-7) or my position (teacher, coordinator, or consultant). When I discovered my good friend, Anita Bibeau, grew milkweed in her garden in order to photograph them, the idea for this book was hatched! We wanted pictures with few words so that readers and non-readers, and those with or without Monarchs, could experience being a scientist—observing, hypothesizing, comparing, contrasting, critically analyzing—all at their own level, with their own vocabulary. We wanted adults to have the information they needed to feel comfortable working with children—and be able to choose how much to share. We wanted every child, no matter the age, to create a product that was guaranteed to be successful—yet so beautiful that parents would keep it on their coffee table for years! We wanted to let you know what clues to look for, so as not to miss the major events of metamorphosis. (Sometimes we stayed up all night, only to fall asleep at the critical time!) Entomology books typically show drawings. We show pictures—of high quality, showing what happens just before and during these events. We are very pleased with the results, and we loved doing it!

What will this journal give to your children?

We have designed this book to give every child
- **Success** in creating a spectacular scientific journal—a real keeper.
- **Excitement and self-esteem** that comes with "I did this myself!"
- **An intimate nature experience** with miraculous metamorphosis, which fosters respect for all life and appreciation for the awesome beauty of every living thing.

Is it going to be easy to raise Monarchs?

Yes! Start with this book, add a little planning to do this at the right times of the year for your locality, obtain some Monarch eggs or caterpillars from established sources (we give you some names and addresses), get milkweed and a jar for every student, and you have the makings of **the highlight of your curriculum!** As I said, I have been doing this for years *without failure!* The close-up photography in *My Monarch Journal* makes it very easy to see and understand the changes taking place. Monarchs follow a very definite, natural course of events—and following along is easy and fun!

Is the information easy to use and flexible?

Again, this book is designed for you—the busy teacher. Every photograph in the student edition has corresponding easy-to-track background information in the parent-teacher edition. Numbered questions and photos correspond to the same numbered and positioned explanations. And life-size photos on many pages give you an easy comparison to your Monarchs. We have also provided a complete, annotated bibliography including estimated reading levels and our recommendations.

Why are there only questions in the student edition?

Questions direct thought. If answers are immediately provided, the thought process often slows down. By having the questions without answers immediately available, more time is created for deeper thinking. Therefore critical and creative thought is encouraged, all without reading. *My Monarch Journal* encourages guessing—which is a very scientific thing to do. Children should look at their Monarch, look at the pictures, do lots of guessing and even more questioning.

For Parents and Teachers

What age range is this good for?

Everyone loves pictures! The picture section is for anyone at any age. Even kindergartners love to examine and talk about the pictures. So do children in any elementary grade. Junior high school and high school students love the pictures too and can go more deeply into it. The background information in the parent-teacher edition is intended for older children, parents and teachers.

Are your children too young for fancy scientific words?

The questions in the student edition only occasionally use scientific words, and they are all defined in the context of the corresponding parent-teacher background information. Later mention of these words is sometimes in parentheses, with more common words substituted. This presentation of words allows you choices—including ignoring them! The glossary is available as a reference tool.

How can I know when the changes will happen?

The pictures in *My Monarch Journal* give you the clues as to when an event is about to occur. I recommend that you appoint a rotating "Monarch Monitor" to "stand watch" for a few minutes at a time (a button, hat or crown adds to the fun) to ensure that nobody misses the drama. We identify what will take place and what to look for to get ready. This means that *you will be there* to see it happen!

How accurate is this book?

I was surprised at how many books, especially books for children, present inaccurate information. Therefore we have provided both the actual photographs and have consulted an entomologist to ensure our information is accurate—at least as much as scientists know at this time.

Write and draw in this book!

It is important for children to have the experience of being a scientist, and keeping a journal, just the way scientists do. Encourage children to write, color and draw in the space provided. This is their book, and Monty is theirs, too!

So you don't have a Monarch of your own?

We would like every young scientist to have a Monarch to raise, but if this is not possible, *My Monarch Journal* provides the next best thing: an opportunity to draw or write about our extraordinary, close-up photographs. A child (of any age!) can still appreciate the remarkable series of events in the life of a Monarch—truly a miracle of metamorphosis.

Do you have more questions?

We want *My Monarch Journal* to be a great resource for you. Please feel free to send your comments and questions to me, in care of the publisher.

Sincerely,

Connie Muther

33

The Egg Hatches (See page 4)

A. What's the little white bump?

No, it's not a leaf wart, or bird droppings. It's an egg laid by a Monarch butterfly! It is smaller than the head of a pin (see the life-size picture in the corner with the head of a pin next to the egg). Magnification is needed.

B. What a funny place for an egg! Why put it there?

A Monarch has a very special relationship with milkweed plants. Mama Monarch lays her eggs right on the food that her baby will eat. These eggs are always found on milkweed leaves, usually on the underside of a small, tender new leaf near the top of the plant. This picture shows the "common milkweed," the most abundant kind in the northeast U.S., which has many tiny hairs on the underside of the leaf. Other varieties may look different.

C. How is it changing?

During the days before your caterpillar hatches, there is a gradual change in the egg color from a pearly white, to creamy yellow, and finally to gray with a black dot on top. This black dot is your baby caterpillar's head inside its egg case. When this dot turns completely black and starts moving, hatching usually begins within 1 to 4 hours.

D. A head pops out! Hello world!

If you're looking with a hand lens, you may even see its tiny head poke through, then move back and forth, creating tiny holes in a row. The caterpillar munches down to enlarge these holes to create an opening. Some caterpillars do this rapidly, others more slowly. Sooner or later it pushes out.

E. How does it get out?

Typically the caterpillar will pause for only a moment, as if startled by its new environment. Some caterpillars then push hard to crawl right out. Others pull back into the egg case and enlarge these holes. **Approximate time to hatch: 1- 3 hours from the first visible pin prick hole in the egg.**

The First Meal (See page 5)

A. What a tight squeeze!

It's a tremendous struggle for your caterpillar to get out of its opening. Your baby caterpillar, called a "hatchling," is so small you can hardly see it! Once out, it may have difficulty walking, because the tiny hairs on the milkweed leaf get in the way. *Note: It is very helpful to have a magnifying glass, hand lens, or microscope. See page 47*

B. What is it doing with the egg case?

The tiny caterpillar may roam a bit, but usually returns to eat the egg case which is thin and easy for tiny jaws to chew, as well as nutritious. Its next meal is often the fuzzy hairs on the underside of the milkweed leaf. It rests a lot.

C. Did it make those holes?

About eight hours after hatching, its jaws are strong enough to eat pockets out of the green leaf between the leaf veins, creating dimples that may bleed a little white sap from the leaf. The green center of the leaf between veins and nearest the stem is more tender than the hard outside edge of a leaf, so that's usually where you'll find your caterpillar. Watch for tiny black droppings, and little holes eaten in leaves—two good ways to tell that it is still there.

D. Oh-oh! Is that little dark blob what I think it is? And why is its body green?

The tiny black blob on the left is "frass," which is the name scientists use for poop! The caterpillar is still translucent, so with magnification you might even see its first green meal travel through its body. The light colored part of its body is where the green meal used to be—where this poop came from. You're watching our caterpillar's intestines work!

E. Is it a boy or a girl? Nobody knows! We named ours Monty. Have you named yours?

There is no way to tell between a "he" and a "she" caterpillar. You will have to wait until it's a butterfly to find out. (Actually, although we are calling our caterpillar Monty, there are several different caterpillars in these pictures. Sometimes important events occurred when we weren't looking—like in the middle of the night—so we had to have several caterpillars.)

The Hatchling Grows (See page 6)

A. Wow! How can she grow so fast?

While you have a skeleton made up of bones that grow slowly and help to hold you up and give your body its shape, Monty has no bones. Instead she has an **exo**skeleton, or skeleton on the outside, made of outer skin. The outer skin is hard and cannot stretch, but some parts of it are folded over like an accordion, which unfold as the caterpillar grows.

B. Look, her face is different! What is that black thing?

When Monty has outgrown her skin, she must get rid of her entire suit of skin (exoskeleton). The scientific word for when an animal sheds its skin, scales, feathers or fur is "molting." On Day 3 Monty molted, and this picture shows her new head. What a difference! The black dot is the discarded covering of her smaller head. It's called a "head capsule." When your caterpillar is bigger and easier to observe, you might be able to see it molting. But it's very difficult to catch when it's happening! We have pictures of Monty doing this later on.

C. How big is Monty now?

It's very hard to measure a young caterpillar. We placed a small centimeter ruler very carefully beside Monty. Be careful—it's easy to hurt a caterpillar. After measuring your caterpillar, go to page 30 and record its size. Watch how fast it grows!

D. What are those floppy things on her body?

Those four long, floppy, velvety black things—two behind her head and two on her rear end—are tentacles. Scientists aren't sure of their purpose, but do know that they are used to brush flies and other pests away, warn birds away, and for camouflage. What do you think they're for? Tentacles are not the same as antennae. Antennae are always on the head, and they feel, taste and smell. Monarch caterpillars have tiny antennae on either side of the mouth. As butterflies, Monarchs have antennae that *look* very much like tentacles, but they are not!

Eating, Pooping, Walking–and Swinging! (See page 7)

A. How much does Monty eat?

Monty, like all Monarch caterpillars, is an eating machine! An average caterpillar will devour 20 to 30 milkweed leaves, about an entire plant, during its life as a caterpillar, which is usually about two weeks. During that time it grows 25 times longer and almost 3000 times heavier than when born. Caterpillars are "cold-blooded" animals which means their blood, called body fluid, changes with the temperature of the surrounding air. Caterpillars develop faster in warm, humid weather than cold, dry weather.

B. Oh-oh! Does she poop much?

Yes—nearly as much as she eats! In the wild, it will fall to the ground to fertilize the soil. In captivity, however, poop can spoil, so clean the cage once a day to keep your caterpillar healthy. Cleaning regularly will also help you notice when your caterpillar is preparing to shed its skin—it stops pooping!

C. How can she walk upside-down?

Caterpillars have no trouble walking upside-down because some of their feet are wide and fleshy, with claw-like hooks called "crochets," so named because they act like a crochet hook. They curve outward, not like a cat's claws that hook inward. Your caterpillar walks upside-down by rolling these special hooks under tiny milkweed hairs and the silk thread that it is always spinning.

D. Does she ever fall off?

Yes. Sometimes caterpillars get knocked off, or deliberately drop off the leaf to escape a predator. If the caterpillar is still small, its silk thread is strong enough to hold its weight. If it is an older, heavier caterpillar, the silk thread breaks, and the caterpillar must find its way back to a milkweed plant. At the base of a caterpillar's mouth is a spinneret which produces delicate but strong silk. Monarchs spin this sticky silk thread wherever they go—like Hansel and Gretel, they can follow it home.

Preparing to Molt (See page 8)

A. Can you make out a new head under Monty's skin?

A caterpillar's new skin grows underneath the old skin. When it is about to molt, the caterpillar's body releases a molting fluid that gradually separates the two layers of skin. The molting fluid also dissolves the inner layers of the old skin, making it thinner and just as clear as plastic wrap. Looking through the clear striped window of Monty's old head covering, you can see the newly separated head inside. This picture shows Monty in the process of pulling her head out and back. This happens very slowly, for about two hours. Her mouth parts, however, remain within the old head covering.

B. Can you see wrinkled new skin under her old skin?

Through the clear thin old skin, the new skin, all wrinkled like a deflated balloon, is visible with magnification. In another three to four hours you will be able to see hair darkening on this wrinkled new skin. During this time, caterpillars inflate, rock and contract. They actually suck in air and pump caterpillar blood (body fluid) into different parts of the body to help it expand, stretching the old skin. They expand and stretch five to 10 times, then rest a few minutes, then repeat the cycle many times.

C. More changes to her head!

For many hours prior to molting you will see the yellow stripes of her new head and the two black shiny spots over her new head. When the "mask" vanishes from across her head, molting has begun. If you are using a microscope with your caterpillar, when you can see hair darkening on its face it is a sign that molting will begin in an hour or two.

Getting Out of the Old Skin (See page 9)

A. Stretch! Watch Monty and her friend below.

When the inflating, rocking, stretching and contracting is continuous for several minutes, the skin begins to move down her body before it splits. (You can tell it has not split yet because she is still wearing her "mask.")

B. She bursts out!

Suddenly, with one straining stretch, the old skin breaks just above and in back of her head. Her new pale yellow head bursts out, leaving the old hardened head covering still attached at her mouth. She continues expanding and stretching, forcing the old skin to slide down. Underneath, her new skin is still wet with molting fluid.

C. What's that gray line?

Notice the gray horizontal line that appears along her sides below her tentacles. These are breathing tubes (tracheae) being pulled out of her body! They are attached to breathing holes (spiracles) located along the sides of her body.

D. How many legs does she have now?

Monty has two different kinds of legs, 16 legs in total. We will examine them more closely later. One by one, or as pairs, they are pulled free of the old skin. The old leg coverings continue to move down with her old skin, creating the illusion that she has even more legs!

E. Watch as she pulls out each wobbly, wet leg!

Molting must be something like wriggling out of a body suit complete with rubber boots. The new legs are wet and wobbly, but she's still able to use them to pull out of her old skin (exoskeleton). It takes about an hour for the new skin to dry and completely harden. Meanwhile Monty continues to suck in air and expand her new skin suit. She needs this new outside skeleton to dry and harden as large as possible.

Finally Free! (See page 10)

A. Finally! Now, watch Monty's head capsule.

The last pair of legs is the most difficult to free. She moves her rear end way out in a final effort to get free. It's a good thing she attached the bottom of her feet to the silk threads on the leaf! The entire process, from when the skin at the head first splits to finally getting free, takes only two to five minutes!

B. "A new me!"

With her old head covering still attached, she moves forward, away from the old skin. At the same time she scrapes her head covering off against the leaf or stem. Once off, she usually moves away from that too. Dust, hair or other small particles touching her new, wet skin might stick to it.

C. Here is the old head covering.

If you wish to examine her head covering more closely, an easy way to pick it up is by touching it with the tip of a thin moistened paintbrush or tightly rolled paper towel. In this picture we've included a pin so you can see how small it is.

The Molted Skin—Yum! (See page 11)

A. Why are Monty's tentacles shaped like Z's?

Tentacles cannot grow because they are confined by the exoskeleton. Yet with each new molt these tentacles double in size. How can something twice as big fit inside the old tentacle coverings? We think the new tentacles are folded up like an accordion, or a Z shape, within the old tentacle covering. Right after molting the new tentacles are still partly folded, but they straighten as they dry. This is our guess. What's yours?

B. What can you see in this old skin?

From a distance the old (molted) skin might be mistaken for a dead fly. Under a magnifying glass it looks like a pile of black and white striped pajamas. The yellow color is gone. (Where did it go?) But leave this old skin—she's not finished with it yet! You may notice the two different kinds of legs she has, the six shiny black claw-like feet and all the fat feet she has, too. We'll talk more about her feet soon.

C. Turning around and . . .

Parts of a caterpillar's skin dry harder than others. The hardest parts are the face, legs and jaws. A caterpillar can't walk very well—or eat—until these parts dry and harden. Monty is turning around. Her legs are strong now. Her jaws are hard. Pass the milkweed, please!

D. Yum!

Instead of milkweed, though, her first meal after molting is usually her old skin! Most people never see a caterpillar molt. Consider yourself lucky if you do. If you miss it with your caterpillar, examine our pictures. It took us a lot of time, patience and luck to make them!

37

The Body Parts (See page 12)

A. Insects have 3 body parts—head, thorax and abdomen. Where are they?

All insects have three body parts: head, thorax (which is like a chest), and abdomen. The wings and legs of an insect are attached to the thorax.

B. How many legs does she have?

Monty has 16 legs—sort of. Really, only the six front ones are "true" legs. See how Monty is holding the milkweed flower? You can see her six claw-like legs, three on each side. However, because she has such a long abdomen, she also has 10 short, thick "false legs" called "prolegs" to hold it up. The prolegs are "false" because they will disappear when she becomes a butterfly. One way to remember the word "prolegs" is to think of them as "prop legs" because they "prop up" the abdomen.

C. Does Monty have no privacy?

Sorry. We were trying to get a good look at that last pair of prolegs, called anal prolegs. Monty kicks them out every time she poops. You will see later that they are very important.

D. How many of Monty's "noses" can you see in this picture?

This is a trick question! Caterpillars don't have noses. They breathe through 18 round holes, nine on each side, called spiracles. The spiracles run along both sides of her long body. They are hard to see because they are usually hidden in a black stripe. How many can you find?

E. Can you find her last air hole? Can you find the hooks on her rear feet?

To find her last air hole (spiracle), locate her rear tentacle and follow it down to the black stripe. It looks like a shiny black port-hole. Once you find it, look at other pictures and see if you can see spiracles. Can you find the tiny hooks on her rear feet? Do you remember what scientists call them? (Crochets.)

Let's Face It–I'm Cute! (See page 13)

A. Can you see her eyes?

On each cheek are six dots the size of pin pricks. These are her eyes! She has 12, six on each side. They are "simple eyes"—very different from the eyes she will have as a butterfly. With 12 eyes, you would think she could see very well, but scientists think she has very poor eyesight and can only distinguish large from small and light from dark. Caterpillars can also distinguish light from dark through their skin! Can you?

B. Can you find her antenna?

Remember—those long black tentacles on the upper part of her body are not antennae! To find Monty's antenna, follow the yellow stripe on her head down to a white and black striped pointed thing. That is an antenna. There is one on each side of her head. She uses it to smell, and perhaps also to taste and feel.

C. Smile, Monty!

It is very hard to see Monty's teeth, which are attached to her jaws (mandibles) that chomp from side to side, just the opposite of what your jaws and teeth do. She has a total of 10 teeth, five on each side. In the next picture you can see two things called "maxillary palps" that stick out from either side of her mouth, which she uses to push food into her mouth. (In the picture they appear to be just below the antenna).

D. Can you find the place that produces her silk?

At the bottom of her head, in the center and pointing down below the maxillary palps, you can see a funnel-shaped organ. This is her spinneret—the organ that is constantly spinning her silk thread. The spinneret produces two liquids which, when they are squirted out, combine with air to create a sticky silk thread—kind of like crazy glue. This is the same kind of silk a silk worm spins, but Monty produces only a little bit of silk whereas silk worms produce huge amounts.

E. What parts can you see in this molted head covering?

It may be easier to see her spinneret by examining a molted head covering—it's the pointed thing on the bottom of the head. If you look carefully, you may be able to identify other parts of her head in this picture. It's fun to use a magnifying glass, hand lens or microscope to examine an old head covering from your caterpillar. You can pick the head coverings up with a thin wet paint brush, as we did in the photo.

How Old Is Your Caterpillar? (See page 14)

Caterpillar growth is affected by temperature and humidity. They develop much faster in warm, moist air than in cool or dry air. Some are in the caterpillar stage for only nine days while others may take as long as 20! Because it is not particularly useful to say how "old" a caterpillar is in terms of days, you might want to guess which "instar" your caterpillar is in—first through fifth. (Please note that this is not easy and is probably better approached as a guessing game than an attempt to be accurate.) Monarch caterpillars come in five sizes called instars, as indicated by the following diagram.

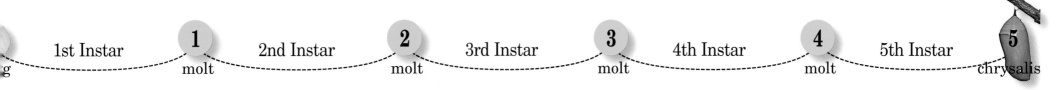

| 1st Instar | **1** | 2nd Instar | **2** | 3rd Instar | **3** | 4th Instar | **4** | 5th Instar | **5** |
| g chrysalis | molt | | molt | | molt | | molt | | chrysalis |

To identify which instar a caterpillar is, scientists look for four things: (1) size of the front tentacles, (2) length of the body, (3) markings on the head and face , and (4) width of the head. For a chart that details the instar differences for each of these factors, please refer to the instar chart on page 49, and compare the differences in the pictures on page 14.

Roaming and Spinning (See page 15)

A. Why did Monty leave the milkweed and start wandering all over?

Now that Monty is fully grown (caterpillars are usually fully grown at 24 to 64 mm long, or 1 to 2 1/2 inches) she suddenly stops eating and begins to roam. She leaves the milkweed plant—the only world she has ever known! She might spend hours, or as long as two days, roaming around. Inside her body, a chemical change has begun. Her time as a caterpillar is almost over.

B. Dead end! What is she looking for?

Monty is looking for a safe place, protected from the sun, wind and rain, and hidden from her enemies. Too much of any one of these could cause her serious injury. She is also looking for a spacious place where she can hang down the whole length of her body and have enough space on all sides to spread her new wings. In captivity, caterpillars often revisit the same spot several times before settling down. Monty is determined to find the perfect spot. How does she know what to do? Scientists don't know!

C. Finally, she stopped—and can you see what she's woven around the twig?

She has only a limited amount of time before her chemicals change so much that she will be unable to crawl. When she's found the ideal spot, she'll stop and rest. Then her head and upper body (thorax) move from side to side, up, down and around in circles. She's spinning her sticky silk thread all over the twig, creating a mat.

D. Can you see what she's doing now?

When the silk mat is firmly attached, she weaves a small white clump in the center, like a tiny lump of cotton candy, which we call a "button." It usually takes three to six hours for her to create both the mat and button.

Creating a White "Button" (See page 16)

A. She's being really fussy about her white button!

This button will be the only way she stays attached to the branch. It must be very secure.

B. Checking it over— it passes inspection!

C. Turning around on a narrow branch . . .

D. "I know that button's there somewhere."

When she's finished spinning, she rests, and then turns around to find the button with her rear legs (anal prolegs). Notice that she's releasing one final poop before grasping her button. She looks funny as she repeatedly lifts her rear end in the air and tries to find her button. She uses the special hooks (crochets) on the inside of her back legs to latch on tightly to her silk button.

E. Hold on, Monty!

Once found, she wriggles to ensure the hooks (crochets) are fully secured. This is a close-up view of her rear legs (anal prolegs) on the button. Notice the silk strands attaching the button securely to the branch.

Letting Go! (See page 17)

A. How many feet are holding on?

After a few hours, with her rear legs (anal prolegs) firmly attached to her button, Monty begins to release her other feet. Sometimes caterpillars will release only one foot at a time; sometimes they release a pair at a time.

B. How many now?

Occasionally, the special tiny hooks (crochets) on a caterpillar's other feet become entangled with the silk, keeping them from swinging free. Most caterpillars release this middle pair of feet last. When Monty tried to release her remaining middle foot, it wouldn't let go.

C. She pushes her head against the branch and . . . whee!

So, she lifted her head and bumped against the branch to jar it loose—and down she swung. How would you feel about letting go, even if your feet were securely anchored?

Last Hours as a Caterpillar (See page 18)

A. How long will Monty hang by her feet?

After more wiggling up and down, she finally rests in a position that looks like a "J." She will "rest" like this for many hours—Monty stayed like this for almost 18 hours. Her mouth moved, as if chewing. Otherwise she appeared to be asleep—but actually her inside organs are already changing from those of a caterpillar to those of a butterfly. Her butterfly antennae, eyes, mouth, legs, and even wings are already growing.

B. She is within 1 to 2 hours of a big change! Do you see what happened?

At first, the only difference you may observe is that the skin near her head is becoming more green. The first big clue, however, is that the long front tentacles shrivel and dry out. As soon as you see this, set a timer and check her every 15 minutes. She will change within one to two hours!

C. She is within 2 to 30 minutes of the big change! What else is happening?

Your caterpillar will change within a half hour when: **(1)** the head drops and the body appears more like an "L;" **(2)** the rear tentacles shrivel up just as the front ones have done; **(3)** the prolegs begin to get smaller and withdrawn into the body; **(4)** the rear legs, attached to the button, seem to get longer; **(5)** the mouth stops moving (what looks to be chewing, but is not) and it stretches its head forward, straining.

D. Where is her head now?

Then her head drops down even farther, actually joining the thorax to form a bulge. Contractions ripple up though her body. This rippling continues as her prolegs seem to pull in even more and all but disappear.

E. Where are her legs going? What's that long line on her side?

In fact, the prolegs are disappearing. Remember, these "false legs" were needed to hold up her long caterpillar abdomen. She will never need them as a butterfly! The long lines on her sides are breathing tubes (tracheae) being pulled out from inside her body through her breathing holes (spiracles). On pages 8 and 9, you saw a similar thing happening in one of her previous molts.

The Last Molt (See page 19)

A. Her skin splits!

Moments later, stretched to its maximum, the skin splits directly behind her head and thorax, and a tiny slice of the newly forming chrysalis is revealed.

B. This molt is like taking off a body suit . . .

As the chrysalis forms, more and more of the caterpillar skin is forced up.

C. with no hands . . .

When the old skin is almost to the top where the button is attached to her rear legs (anal prolegs), look for a black dot to appear. It signals that a shiny black rod will poke out. This rod is called a cremaster.

D. while hanging from your legs . . .

She will hang from the branch by this cremaster instead of her rear legs (anal prolegs). The cremaster has hooks on its tip, all pointing in different directions. She must reach over the old skin and maneuver the tip of her cremaster, with all those miniature hooks, into her silk button. This is critical!

E. then changing shoes! (How is she attached to the white "button" now?)

She stops all contractions briefly until she finds the button, then jabs the tip of the cremaster into it. It will stick like Velcro. Then she twists and turns, both to entangle the hooks more securely and to jostle off the remnants of her old caterpillar skin.

Becoming a Chrysalis (See page 20)

A. How can Monty get rid of her dirty laundry?

Twisting and turning, almost like dancing, Monty gyrates, seemingly frantic to get all the old skin off. Whatever touches her new, wet skin may become embedded. For only a minute or two you can see the complete outline of her new butterfly antennae, legs and eyes. Her new mouth parts run right down the center.

B. Is it a caterpillar? Or a butterfly?

How long can you see it as a caterpillar? How soon can you see it as a butterfly? The shape of the wings is forming before your eyes.

C. How long does it take?

In a little more than one hour the final chrysalis shape is achieved. The newly formed chrysalis is pale yellow and blue-green. You will also see a black, yellow and white band and several yellow spots. Monarchs are extremely vulnerable right now. Even a blowing leaf could slice into it. Be very careful not to touch your chrysalis. It usually takes another 15 to 20 hours for the new chrysalis skin (cuticle) to harden, at which time the yellow spots turn to gold.

The Chrysalis–Beautiful and Intriguing (See page 21)

A. Why does it have gold spots and a gold band?

Nobody knows why a chrysalis has this "jewelry." Some scientists think it helps camouflage the chrysalis. Others think it acts as a light and temperature sensor. One scientist (Urquart, see bibliography) carefully cut away the gold coloring without harming the chrysalis. The emerging butterflies did not have bright colors on their wings. He concluded that the light passing through the gold somehow imparts color to the scales.

B. Monty is "X-rayed" with sunlight for a minute. How does she breathe?

You can "X-ray" your chrysalis with sunlight or a strong light. But be very careful! If left in the sun or near a lamp too long, it may overheat and die. After the chrysalis is a few days old, you will see body parts forming. Can you find Monty's breathing holes (spiracles)? In the previous picture, locate the end of the gold band. Four holes are above it and two are below it.

C. How can Monty live without eating?

The new butterfly cells are growing and being nourished by decomposing caterpillar cells. How did Monty eat as a caterpillar? Will she eat the same way as a butterfly? Will she even eat the same food? Everything except her circulatory and respiratory systems is changing—a true metamorphosis. Monty has had three forms so far: egg, caterpillar (with 16 legs, including prolegs,), and now a chrysalis (with no legs)! Think of all the changes!

D. Where are her legs, mouth, and head now?

This photo, backlit with sunlight, shows Monty's developing head, antennae, legs and tongue (proboscis). A Monarch chrysalis begins to change color two days before a butterfly emerges. It is usually in the chrysalis form for about seven to 13 days.

E. Her color is changing! Can you see the wings? Tomorrow is the big day!

The day before Monty emerged, her entire chrysalis turned a darker gray-green. You can see her wings more clearly now because the scales on her wings are getting their color. Orange and black begins to show through the transparent wall of her chrysalis.

A Butterfly Is Born (See page 22)

A. Now she's black and orange! Why?

Monty became orange and black several hours before emerging with orange and black wings. The scales on her wings can be seen clearly because they are still attached to the chrysalis casing.

B. Do you see the notched grooves that have formed? It's time to watch closely!

The notched grooves just above the gold band mean Monty is ready to get out! Set a timer to watch every few minutes. She will emerge within one to two hours after these notched grooves appear. Examine the abdominal area above the wing tips up to the cremaster. She is separating from her chrysalis skin. Compare this picture with the previous one. See how cloudy it is—especially in the area of the spiracles.

C. The casing splits!

The chrysalis casing first splits directly behind her head. You may have to lie on your back and look up, or experiment with a mirror in order to see this. Looking up, if you are lucky and patient, you will see the split appear first as a light gray line, then turn black as the hairs on her body poke through it.

D. How does she get out?

Her head drops down while her feet remain hooked inside the chrysalis. She pauses for a few seconds, then pushes forward as she continues to drop down. If you look very carefully, you can see Monty's legs, antennae and long tongue (proboscis) still attached inside the chrysalis. Monarchs emerge differently, so don't worry if your Monarch does not come out exactly as Monty did. Usually the head drops down while feet remain hooked inside the chrysalis.

The Emerging Monarch (See page 23)

A. Almost out . . .

Monty drops down, leaving a trail of white lines still attached to the chrysalis casing. These are her long breathing tubes (tracheae) again being pulled out from her breathing holes (spiracles). She continues to breathe through these spiracles as an adult butterfly.

B. Monty, are your feet stuck?

Amazingly, the whole weight of her body is supported by her feet which are still anchored inside her chrysalis casing.

C. Are her wings on backwards?

Her wings are still folded over. What you could see through the chrysalis was the bright outer side of her wing. As a butterfly, this brilliant orange color will be hidden on the inside when she closes her wings, and beautifully displayed when she opens them.

D. Her body is kind of fat, and her wings are kind of short!

Her body is very fat right now. And her wings measure only 20 mm (less than an inch). But not for long!

43

The Home Stretch (See page 24)

A. Why is Monty so fat?

Her new butterfly body (abdomen) is thick and wide because it is filled with body fluid. Her wings are small because they hardly have any. But this changes before your eyes, like magic!

B. Are those wires coming out of her mouth?

What appears to be a long tongue is actually a sucking tube (proboscis), like a straw. When it is growing inside the chrysalis, it is separated into two halves, like a straw sliced lengthwise. Monty must join these two halves together by means of special latches on the tubes' edges, which work like a zipper. Her new mouth, now without teeth or jaws, is at the base of the proboscis. No more milkweed—from now on, she's on a liquid diet of water and flower nectar!

C. Wow! How do her wings grow so fast?

Watch as she squeezes her body (abdomen) up and then relaxes. She is forcing body fluid into her wing veins. You can see most of these veins in the middle of the black lines along her wings. Her wings begin to expand and unfold. The fluid is pumped into her wing veins, unfolding them like those party toys you blow into and roll out. As her wings expand, her abdomen shrinks.

D. Are wings kind of like kites?

Butterfly wings are very much like kites. Once they are fully expanded, some of the body fluid used to pump up the wings is sucked back into the body; the rest will evaporate, leaving hard, dry hollow tubes that look like veins. These "veins" support the wings like the struts on a kite. This is why, in captivity, it is so important that your butterfly be able to emerge where it can fully extend its wings. Otherwise, it may dry deformed and never fly.

E. When can Monty fly?

Monty cannot fly until her wings are fully unfolded, dried and hardened. It took only 10 minutes for her wings to fully unfold, but it will take one to two hours for them to dry and harden. During this time, it's fun to examine her closely. After her wings are expanded, you'll find reddish stuff below her. This is the waste created while she was in her chrysalis.

Examining Your New Butterfly (See page 25)

A. How many wings does Monty have?

As Monty dries she begins to expand her wings a little. You can count four wings, two on each side. Butterflies stay quiet while their wings are drying, so this is an excellent time to take a good look. You have about two hours. Notice the liquid at the base of her abdomen. Now her "poop" is liquid.

B. Can you count her toes?

At the end of her new legs are a set of needle-sharp claws with which she can hook into microscopic nooks and crannies that the human eye cannot see. Hanging on tightly is important, because unless in captivity, she may emerge on a windy day. If she falls to the ground before her wings have expanded and dried, she could be critically damaged.

C. Her eyes are very different!

Do you remember the 12 tiny "simple eyes" she had as a caterpillar? Now look! Monty has two large "compound" eyes, each composed of thousands of tiny parts, each allowing her to see in a slightly different direction. She can now detect color and movement, and see in all directions except directly underneath her.

D. Look at the long wires attached to her head!

These are Monty's antennae—very different from her caterpillar antennae. They are very sensitive. They are how she hears, tastes and smells, letting her know where to fly. Butterflies can taste in four places: antennae, mouth, feet, and even on the hind end!

E. Let's look closer. Can you find her scales?

Butterflies have modified hairs called scales and only a little hair. Scales are like shingles on a roof, overlapping each other and adding strength. Look carefully at your butterfly and ask lots of questions: How does it fly? Where does it go? Can it do math? Does it catch a cold? What does it do at night? Sometimes you can find answers in books. See page 51 for a bibliography of the books we think are best. However, we still do not know the answers to many of our questions.

Releasing Your Butterfly (See page 26)

A. Finally we can tell—is Monty a boy or girl?

Monty is a girl. Females have wider black lines on their wings.

B. Here's a boy—what is distinctive about him?

An even better way of telling the difference between the sexes is that only males have two black dots, which are scent glands, on their wings.

C. Can you find Monty's new head, thorax and abdomen?

Remember, the thorax has six legs and wings attached. Monty appears to have only four legs. Hidden beneath her head is another pair of legs that are so hard to see that we couldn't get a good photograph of them. Monarch caterpillars don't seem to use them. Nobody knows what they do. As with all insects, however, there are six legs!

D. When and how should I release my butterfly?

After an hour or two, it's time to set it free. Place your finger gently in front of it and press toward its body; your butterfly should step onto your finger. Hold your other hand beneath it in case it falls, because its wings are still limp and it cannot fly. Carefully carry it outside and place it in front of a branch. With your hand still underneath, gently roll your finger so it has to take a step. It will fly when it's ready. In case of rain, release in a sheltered spot.

E. Goodbye Monty! I wonder where she will go?

Monarch butterflies usually live for a few weeks in summer, but for many months in winter. Monty and your Monarch may take a trip of thousands of miles, and join many other Monarchs. Some will eventually return home, or their offspring will. How can that be? How will they know where to go? Scientists who study Monarchs have been asking these questions for years. Some answers they found are in books, or in articles on the internet.

Milkweed–for Breakfast, Lunch and Dinner (See page 27)

A. Milkweed is the only thing Monarch caterpillars eat! What does it look like?

The Monarch caterpillar eats only milkweed plants. Milkweed is a non-branching plant with pairs of leaves growing out from opposite sides of the stem. This is a picture of "common milkweed" which grows in the northeastern U.S. and eastern Canada. It may not look like the kind of milkweed that grows near you. There are 2,400 different kinds of milkweed that grow around the world—and maybe more that haven't been discovered yet!

B. What is that white drop?

When you snap off a leaf, a milk-white sap trickles out. This is why it is called "milk" weed and is one of the ways to identify it. In summer the common milkweed has a large flower cluster that turns into a light green pod. In the fall, as the plant dries, this pod turns gray and bursts open, releasing its seeds attached to white, feathery parachutes that blow with the wind.

C. Where can I find it?

Look for the pods in fall and winter—then you will know where to go in the summer. Look for milkweed in dry, sunny places. It usually grows in fields among other weeds. In the city you may find it pushing through cracks in tar or cement. It grows by the sides of buildings, in vacant lots, or near fences. In the country, it is frequently found in pastures because cows dislike its taste and leave it alone.

D. How can I grow it? How can I keep it?

You can grow milkweed from seed, or it can be transplanted to your garden with care. First notice where you find your plant—dry or wet, sunny all day or partially shady? Find a similar spot for it. Dig deep around and under it to ensure you get all the roots. Transplant only one or two plants at a time, to see if they thrive in their new location. If you do not have milkweed close by, you can cut a stalk, place the stem in water and it will be fine for about a week. If it's late in the season and there may be a frost, pick off enough leaves for your caterpillars and freeze them in plastic bags.

45

Following are answers to the questions posed on pages 28 and 29—plus a few more questions and answers.

A. When—and how—can I find Monarch eggs or caterpillars?

You can find Monarch eggs and caterpillars from April through October most anywhere in the United States or Canada that has milkweed. You must have access to milkweed! First, find a milkweed plant. Look at the entire plant before touching it.

- Look for tiny, fresh circular holes in the center of the leaves—a sign of newly hatched caterpillars.
- Look for poop on any of the leaves.
- Look to see whether the edges of any leaves have been recently eaten—a sign of bigger caterpillars.

If you don't see any of these clues, begin at the top of the milkweed plant, looking closely at each leaf, especially the underside. Typically, this is where Monarchs will lay a single egg. Systematically work your way down the plant, turning over each leaf. If you think you've found something, carefully break the leaf off to examine it more carefully. It helps to have a copy of this book so you can compare what you find with our pictures. Place whatever you find in a container to carry. If you don't have a container with you, hold one hand beneath the leaf that holds your egg or caterpillar, to protect it should it fall off.

B. What do I do with the eggs? How do I feed it?

When you find a leaf with an egg, put the leaf on a dish. Place a crumpled tissue on top of the stem and moisten it with water. Make sure the water level is not near the egg because a newly hatched caterpillar could fall into the water and drown. Compare your egg with the pictures in this book, and you will know about when it will hatch. Since we watch ours closely, we leave them in this dish until they are a few days old. You may wish to put it in a jar right away to protect it—and just in case it decides to wander.

C. How do I pick up my baby caterpillar? Where should I keep it?

Never try to pick up a baby caterpillar! It's too easily hurt. (See page 47, "When Can I Handle My Caterpillar?") You can move it to a new leaf by cutting parts of the old leaf away and placing the old leaf on the new one. Your caterpillar eventually finds the new leaf and crawls onto it. A heavy glass or hard plastic jar (at least four inches tall and three inches wide) makes a good container. Even when dropped, it will rarely break or damage the caterpillar. Place your caterpillar on its milkweed leaf inside. Punch many holes in the top for air. (To put holes in plastic lids, use a heated ice pick.) Another good lid is netting that is tied on. Your caterpillar doesn't like to be disturbed and will stop moving if jostled, so keep the jar right on your desk or table while you work. Then you can peek at your caterpillar without bothering it. Be sure to keep this journal nearby, so you can record what you see! *WARNING: Caterpillars will overheat if the jar is left in the sun and will stop growing if left near an air conditioner.*

D. How often should I clean the cage? What should I look for?

Keep your caterpillar's container clean! When your caterpillar is large enough for you to see, empty your jar out on a clean white sheet of paper or paper toweling almost every day. Then examine everything: poop, edges of leaves, caterpillar parts. Use a magnifying glass, and you'll find even more. If there's not much poop (frass), it may mean your caterpillar has spent the day preparing to molt. You may even find its head covering and know it has molted—again! This is the best way to know if your caterpillar has molted. If your caterpillar is eating from the edges of the leaf, it may mean its mouth is bigger. What do you find? What does it mean? Scientists look at everything, then they guess. It's fun to guess! Often scientists learn even more from their wrong guesses than they do from their right ones.

E. Measuring—and feeding it more and more!

Be sure to measure your caterpillar when it is large enough and record your findings both in your log and on the growth chart on page 30 of your book. Then put it back in its jar with fresh milkweed. When your caterpillar is very small (only a few days old), it usually stays on one leaf. But it

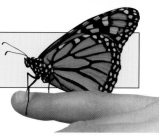

doubles in size almost every day! So expect to add fresh milkweed leaves every day, adding more leaves as it gets older. It should never be without milkweed. You'll be amazed at how fast it grows and how much it eats!

F. Magnifying glasses and hand lenses are fun . . .

Magnifying glasses are helpful but they usually only enlarge two to four times. Hand lenses, which you can buy in a nature store, are even better. Hand lenses enlarge from seven to 15 times the actual size.

G. But stereo microscopes are the best! How can I get one?

Seeing your caterpillar through a stereo (two eye-piece, two objectives) microscope magnifies 30 to 1000 times the actual size! You may obtain these "dissecting" or "inspection" microscopes in nature stores, or from your local high school biology lab or a large scientific company in your town. One source is Insights at 800-942-0528. It's worth borrowing one even if you have access to it for just one day! Children as young as three years old can see through these scopes if an adult sets it up for them.

H. When can I handle my caterpillar?

It's very difficult to pick up or touch tiny caterpillars without hurting them. Wait until your caterpillar is about an inch long and then, if you like, you may let it walk onto your finger. Make sure it is not in the process of molting. If you gently roll the leaf so it is forced to take a step, it will be walking on your finger. Have fun letting it tickle your hand. Monarch caterpillars do not bite. Examine it carefully, and when you are finished, let it crawl back onto a fresh milkweed leaf. Be sure to write your findings in your log!

I. What's the best place for my caterpillar to make a chrysalis?

After nine to 12 days, caterpillars begin to search for a place to become a chrysalis. They must have enough room for their new butterfly form to emerge, hang and then spread its wings to dry. In captivity a Monarch usually chooses the top of any cage and prefers a rough surface, away from light. In the wild they go under overhangs and branches. If we have many caterpillars we put roaming caterpillars in a large container with heavy wire mesh across the top, weighted down with bricks. After the last one has made its chrysalis, we take the wire off and support it between two tall stacks of books. This leaves plenty of room. If your caterpillar has made its chrysalis on the lid of a jar, place the lid between two stacks of books so it has plenty of room to spread its wings. Keep it where it cannot be bumped.

J. How about a large cage?

The cage pictured on page 29 is ideal. You may keep many plants in bottles of water for many days. Some caterpillars will fall off and roam, but they eventually become chrysalises on the top screen. When they emerge, they'll be contained, with plenty of room to fly. And when the project is finished you can dismantle it easily and store it for the following year.

How can I keep my caterpillars fed when they eat so much?

You can keep up to three caterpillars on a milkweed plant in a glass bottle filled with water. To keep them from crawling down into the bottle and drowning, wrap the stem of your plant with a folded paper towel and make sure it fits tightly against the sides of the bottle. Now your caterpillar will have a constant supply of fresh leaves for about a week. Most caterpillars will not crawl down vertical glass. Be sure the bottle is tall and the label is removed, so there are no rough places to crawl down.

How many caterpillars or eggs may I keep in one container?

Some Monarch caterpillars raised in captivity will cannibalize other eggs and hatchlings. This only occurs in crowded cages, never in the wild. Each caterpillar should have its own leaf. Hatchlings rarely leave the leaf they emerge on until after a day or two. We keep one or two caterpillars in one container, and no more than three caterpillars on a plant.

What about predators?

When you prepare your milkweed plants, be sure to check every leaf, especially at the top of the plant; remove any spiders, earwigs or other critters that you find!

A Parent-Teacher Checklist for Raising Monarchs

You do not need to raise Monarchs for this Journal to work! However, it is ideal to do so. Here is a quick checklist for getting started.

❏ If you are unfamiliar with milkweed, call your local Audubon or nature society to help you locate it. See pages 27 and 45.

❏ Obtain a copy of the student edition of *My Monarch Journal* for each child's use. Do so early enough for children to use the book to help locate milkweed.

❏ Obtain eggs or caterpillar hatchlings from Monarch organizations or butterfly farms (or locate in nature) when milkweed is at least a few inches high. See below.

❏ Glass jars and/or a classroom screen cage should be ready before the eggs or caterpillars arrive. See pages 46 and 47.

❏ If possible, obtain magnifying glasses, hand lenses and arrange to borrow an industrial or dissecting stereo microscope from a school biology lab or other source. See page 47.

For the next three to four weeks, observe the Monarchs develop—examine, compare, ask questions, guess! Then encourage your students to color, draw and write observations in *My Monarch Journal.*

Tips for Teachers

How many ways can I use this book?
This book has been designed for multiple uses:
- Use as a science log—with or without Monarch caterpillars, letting students choose to draw or to write their personal observations from the pictures.
- Use as a reference tool.
- Use twice—and have children guess! First prior to raising caterpillars. (Do not share any answers with students. They can't stand not knowing!) Then, as a science log, while each child raises his/her own caterpillar.
- Read the "answers" silently first while students continue to discuss. Then choose what is age appropriate to share. (It gives them more time to think!)
- Give each child his/her completed journal at the end of the year and both you and this Monarch experience will be a positive school experience remembered forever!

How can I order Monarchs?
You can search for Monarch egg sources on the internet. Many commercial sites are listed. There may also be butterfly farms near you. There are five near us! Or, you may purchase Monarch caterpillars and eggs from the two nonprofit organizations. *East of the Rockies:* contact Monarch Watch, 1-888-TAGGING or 1-913-864-4441. Website: www.monarchwatch.org. E-mail: Monarch@ukans.edu. *West of the Rockies:* contact The Monarch Program/ California Monarch Sites, (760) 944-7113. E-mail: Monarchprg@aol.com.

How many caterpillars do I need?
I recommend one caterpillar for each student, plus about 20 extra to raise as a class project. If necessary, the extra caterpillars can be inserted surrepti-tiously into a student's jar if their caterpillar dies or appears sick. I recommend that students keep their jars on their desk or table, labeled with their name and the date they began. Inspect every few days make sure each caterpillar is healthy.

How can I delay things if I need to?
You can delay the growth of your Monarchs at all stages of development by refrigeration in a covered container no longer than a few days. This way you can have several Monarchs in different stages of growth!

Chrysalises on jar lids in the classroom! Help!
When caterpillars make their chrysalises on the top of a jar lid, you may wish to suspend the lids from a tight wire across the ceiling. Simply sew a support through the holes on the lid with strong thread. Suspend each lid, with its attached chrysalis, from the wire. Everyone can watch as each butterfly emerges.

Can I move a chrysalis?
Sometimes a chrysalis needs to be moved. Wait until it is several days old and its casing is thoroughly hardened. Moisten the silk matting. Holding the stem between your fingers, gently but firmly pull the chrysalis and its silk matting away from the surface. Carefully tie a thread around the chrysalis' stem (cremaster), twisting the silk strands from the matting into your knot. Reattach it where it has plenty of room (we use a sturdy branch) to emerge and spread its drying wings. Tie the stem so it will not swirl when your butterfly emerges.

How to Find the "Age" of Your Caterpillar

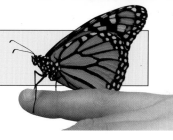

Scientists tell the "age" of a caterpillar by what "instar" it is, rather than how many days old it is, because caterpillars grow at very different rates depending on temperature and humidity. Please see the discussion on the top of page 39, and the pictures on page 14. *It is very difficult to "age" caterpillars accurately, and we recommend that it be approached as a guessing game—for those who wish to attempt it!* We feel the easiest method for young scientists to identify instars is to measure the tentacles, because tentacles do not get longer during an instar. The next best method is to measure body length; but be aware that caterpillars stretch longer during an instar. It is also interesting to examine the head markings. The most reliable method, used by entomologists, is to measure the width of the head capsule. However, it's too tiny for young scientists to measure. On page 14 is a picture of their actual sizes, and in the chart below are approximate head covering measurements for the different instars.

Method of measuring	First instar (hatchling, usually 1-4 days)	Second instar (before 2nd molt, usually 1-3 days)	Third instar (before 3rd molt, usually 1-3 days)	Fourth instar (before 4th molt, usually 2-5 days)	Fifth instar (before 5th molt —chrysalis— usually 2-6 days)
Front tentacles	Too small to measure; don't be fooled by the two black spots between the head and tentacles.	Still too short to measure; the two black spots between the head and tentacles are not as obvious.	Tentacles are 1 to 2 mm long; two black spots are now covered by the first black band behind the head.	Tentacles are 4 to 6 mm long (about 1/4 inch).	Tentacles are 9 to 13 mm long (about 1/2 inch).
Body	2-6 mm long (1/16-1/4 inch) Body is almost transparent with obvious hair; black bands are not distinct.	5-10 mm long (1/4-about 1/2 an inch) Bands and the yellow coloring begin to show; not as much hair.	9-14 mm long (about 1/2 an inch) Yellow bands are clearly distinguished; white "socks" above the shiny black "shoes" are noticeable.	13-25 mm long (1/2 -1 inch) White, yellow and black bands are more vivid; white "socks" are even more distinct.	24-64 mm long (1-2 1/2 inches) Bands widen; stripes are more vibrant; white "socks" diminish and appear more like large dots.
Head markings	Head is black; sometimes you can see a tiny white rectangle above the mouth.	Head has two narrow white stripes around a triangle; white rectangle above the mouth is more visible.	Head has wider stripes, with a more distinct triangle. Usually these stripes are yellow, but may remain white.	Stripes are deep yellow and wider than the black stripes; rectangle above mouth is still white.	Yellow stripes narrow while black stripes broaden; rectangle above mouth is usually yellow.
Head capsule (approximate sizes)	.05 mm wide	.07 mm wide	1.3 mm wide	2.2 mm wide	3.8 mm wide

Reproducible Chart

Events in My Monarch's Life

The Four Stages of Metamorphosis	Typical Events (yours may differ!)	Approximate Time	Event	Time
Egg	Pearl white or creamy yellow Dark gray to black dot of head	**1 to 5 days** **1 to 2 days**		
Caterpillar **First instar** (hatch to 1st molt) **Second instar** (1st to 2nd molt) **Third instar** (2nd to 3rd molt) **Fourth instar** (3rd to 4th molt) **Fifth instar** (4th molt to chrysalis)	For a detailed description of changes in each instar, see chart on page 49.	**2 to 4 days** **1 to 3 days** **1 to 3 days** **2 to 5 days** **2 to 6 days**		
Chrysalis	Hardening of chrysalis Light jade green color Green darkens to black	**12 to 19 hours** **7 to 12 days** **1 to 3 days**		
Butterfly	Emerging to fully unfolded wings First Monarchs of the season live several weeks; migrating Monarchs live several months	**10 to 15 minutes** **weeks to months**		

Reproducible Chart

A Butterfly Bibliography

Author's note: We have included in this journal only the part of the Monarch's life you can see. For answers to the many other questions that will be generated by the experience of watching Monarchs, such as mating, egg laying, and migrating, refer to the resources listed here. Storybooks, even though excellent, are not included unless they also provide accurate scientific information. We have also tried to give a sense of the book's contents, as well as a recommendation and reading level.

Arnosky, Jim, ***Crinkleroot's Guide To Knowing Butterflies & Moths,*** Simon & Schuster Books For Young Readers, 1996. A cartoon character guides children on a journey to learn about moths and butterflies. Information is accurate. Reading level: Grades 1-3.

Brewer, Jo, ***Butterflies,*** Harry N. Abrams, Inc., 1976 A well-written, scientifically accurate presentation of the life of all butterflies with excellent photographs. **Highly recommended**. Reading level: High school to adult

Chinery, Michael, ***Butterfly,*** Troll Assoc., 1991. An excellent, easy to read book about the Tiger Swallowtail butterfly. Photography and drawings are excellent. **Recommended**. Reading level: Grades 2-4.

Conniff, Richard, ***Spineless Wonders (Strange Tales From The Invertebrate World),*** Henry Holt & Co., 1996. Clearly written and entertaining, about the world of creepy boneless creatures. Although factual, this book reads like a novel. **Highly recommended** for those who love this. Reading level: Adult.

Craighead George, Jean, ***The Moon of the Monarch Butterflies,*** Thomas Y. Crowell Co., 1968. Narrative story of the life of a butterfly following its migration. Includes pen and ink illustrations, and describes other animals the butterfly might see. The vocabulary is not controlled. Reading level: Grade 5 and up.

Doris, Ellen, ***Entomology,*** Thames and Hudson Inc., 1993. Subtitled, "With Lots of Adventures, Projects, and Ideas for Exploring the World of...Butterflies, Ants, Dragonflies, Crickets and all the other insects." Excellent information with photos showing activities. **Highly recommended**. Reading level: Grade 5 to adult.

Facklam, Margery, ***Creepy, Crawly Caterpillars***, Little, Brown & Co., 1996. Fun book about several of the most fascinating caterpillars. Excellent illustrations. Four stages pictured with description of each type of caterpillar. Some information is inaccurate, but it's an excellent book. **Recommended**. Reading level: Grades 3-5.

Garland, Peter, ***Monarch Butterfly,*** The Wright Group, 1992. Great photos but they may be misleading. **Highly recommended** for non-readers. Reading level: K-1st grade.

Gibbons, Gail, ***Monarch Butterfly***, Holiday House, 1989. Easy picture book with primitive drawings. One drawing shows a newly hatched butterfly inside a jar; but by doing this you risk constricting the developing wings, creating a deformed butterfly if the jar is not large enough. Reading level: Grade 2.

Goor, Ron and Nancy, ***Insect Metamorphosis: From Egg to Adult,*** Atheneum Macmillan Co., 1990. Focuses on the development of the Hickory Horned Devil Moth. This huge caterpillar hibernates as a pupa underground. Fantastic pictures, simple language. **Highly recommended**. Reading level: Grades 3-4.

Green, Jen, ***Endangered Butterflies***, Benchmark Books, 1999. Text appears accurate but the Monarch chrysalis photo was placed sideways, leading us to question the accuracy of other information. Reading level: Grades 4-5.

Ivy, Bill, ***Monarch Butterfly,*** Grolier Ltd., 1986. Excellent book with outstanding pictures. Written for kids, but any age will enjoy it! **Highly recommended**.

Larcheveque, Lee, ***The Butterfly King,*** Monarch Watch (888-824-4464), 1998, This 20-minute video film shows the growth of the Monarch from egg to adult cleverly using two settings: the wild and a home. Photography is excellent, but leaves the erroneous impression that it takes less time than in reality. Monarch predators, animal and human, are all viewed, with consequences. **Highly recommended**. Viewing level: Any age, but preview because parts may be too graphic for young children.

Lasky, Kathryn, ***Monarchs,*** Harcourt Brace & Co., 1993. Excellent information, great photographs, well written. It is one of the few resources to reveal how the butterfly tongue (proboscis) is in two parts upon emerging from the chrysalis. Most of the book deals with how the butterflies spend the winter and identifying the specific places in Mexico. **Highly recommended**. Reading level: Grades 4 to adult.

Lavies, Bianca, ***Monarch Butterflies Mysterious Travelers,*** Dutton Children's Books, 1992. Excellent information, detailed photographs, well written. Summarizes research of Monarch's migration and overwintering in Mexico. Explores threats of survival and impact of other animals and humans. **Highly recommended.** Reading level: Grades 3 and up.

Lepthien, Emilies, ***A New True Book of Monarch Butterflies,*** Children's Press, 1989. Large print children's book dealing mostly with Monarch migration. Vocabulary is not controlled and writing is not clear. Reading level: Grades 2-3

Marcher, Marion W., ***Monarch Butterfly,*** E.M. Hale & Co., 1960. Pleasant fictional account of the life of a Monarch Butterfly. Simple language. Reading level: Grades 2-3.

Merrick, Patrick, ***Caterpillars***, The Child's World Inc., 1998. The photography in this book is good, but the information is not always accurate. Reading level: Grades 1-3.

Norsgaard, E. Jaediker, ***Butterflies for Kids***, North Word Press, 1996. Two children spend the summer raising butterflies as taught by their nature photographer father. Simple language, beautiful pictures, accurate information; an excellent book to inspire children to write their own stories. **Highly recommended**. Reading level: Grade 3 - adult.

Norsgaard, E. Jaediker, ***How to Raise Butterflies***, Dodd, Mead & Co., 1988. Large print, detailed photographs. Text includes timeframes. Introduces general information as well as how to find the egg, incubate it, types of cages and how to make a habitat. Provides information about other butterflies. One page shows a cage containing numerous caterpillars, a dangerous practice. **Highly recommended**. Reading level: Grades 3 and up.

Oberhauser, Karen and Kuda, Kristen, ***A Field Guide to Monarch Caterpillars,*** National Science Foundation, 1997. This 14-page guide describes the 5 instars. Clear and concise, providing scientific words defined in context. **Highly recommended**. Reading level: High School to adult.

Pringle, Laurence, ***An Extraordinary Life: The Story of a Monarch Butterfly***, Orchard Books, 1997. Narrative of the life of one Monarch from hatching through migration. Information is accurate with excellent paintings. Sidebar information provides additional facts. **Highly recommended**. Reading level: Grade 4 through adult.

Rood, Ronald, ***Answers About Insects,*** Grosser & Dunlap Inc., 1969. Fun, accurate book. Excellent information, clear, simple writing, good illustrations. **Highly recommended**, even though old copyright date. Reading level: Grades 3-4.

Rosenblatt, Lynn M., ***Monarch Magic! Butterfly Activities & Nature Discoveries,*** Williamson Publishing Co., 1998. Clearly written, informative yet simple text describes the entire life cycle of the Monarch including migration routes. Many scientific yet fun projects for kids. **Highly recommended.** Reading level: Grade 3.

Ross, Michael E., ***Caterpillarology,*** Carolrhoda Books, Inc., 1997. Filled with questions, experiments and activities. Well written, accurate information. This book is a must! **Highly recommended.** Reading level: Grades 4-6, but anyone will enjoy it.

Royston, Angela, ***Life Cycle of a Butterfly,*** Heinemann Library, 1998. Simple language; text information is stretched in order to keep it simple. However, it is a good 2nd grade reading book; younger children will enjoy the pictures. Reading level: Grade 2 and under.

Stokes, Donald & Lillian, & Williams, Ernest, ***The Butterfly Book: An Easy Guide to Butterfly Gardening, Identification, and Behavior,*** 1991. Wonderful general reference guide. Terrific pictures. Excellent information for raising different kinds of butterflies and their food. **Highly recommended**. Reading level: High school.

Taylor, Kim. ***Butterfly,*** Dorling Kindersley Publishing, Inc. 1992. A wonderful first grade reader with excellent photographs of the Tiger Swallowtail. Only flaw: at no time are you told what kind of butterfly it is or what it eats. **Highly recommended**. Reading level: Grade 1.

Urquhart, Fred A., ***The Monarch Butterfly: International Traveler,*** Wm. Caxton Ltd,. 1988. Urquhart's highly technical scientific research results are presented in a clear style for the layman. He is the definitive author in the field. This book is our favorite. **Highly recommended**. Reading level: Adult.

Wagner, David L., et al., ***Caterpillars of Eastern Forests***, Forest Service (FHTET-96-34), U.S. Dept. of Agriculture, 1997. This fascinating reference book describes more than 150 forest caterpillars, with incredible photographs. **Highly recommended** for those who really want to get into this! Reading level: Adult.

51

About the Authors

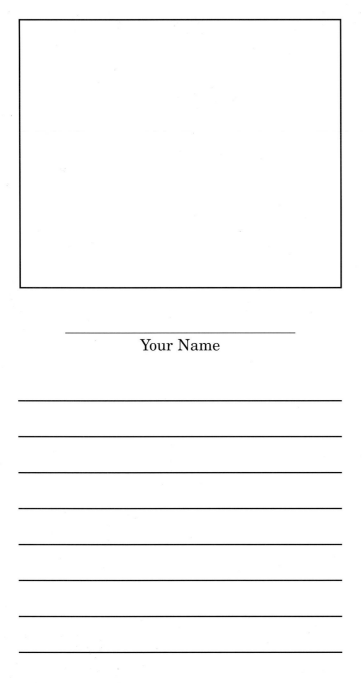

Your Name

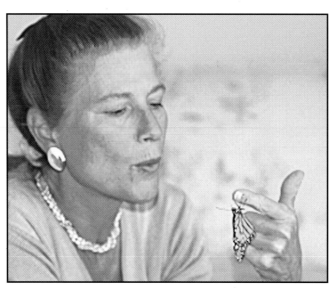

Connie Muther, a former teacher who raised Monarchs in the classroom, is currently an international educational consultant and speaker. She has guided hundreds of school districts in curriculum review and instructional materials selection. She lives in Manchester, Connecticut.

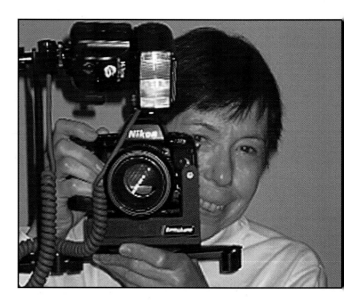

Anita Bibeau is a third-generation photographer whose childhood experiences growing up in rural South Hadley, Massachusetts eventually led her to the love of her life—nature photography. Her mission is to use the magic of photography to communicate the wonder, excitement and awesome beauty of Mother Nature and to inspire others to cherish, nurture and protect Her.